FERRARI
THE LEGEND

by
SHIRLEY HAINES
and
HARRY HAINES

THE ROURKE CORPORATION, INC.
Vero Beach, FL 32964

ACKNOWLEDGMENTS

The authors and publisher wish to thank FERRARI, S.p.A. for invaluable assistance in compiling the photographs and technical information for this book. Special thanks are due Maurizio Parlato for locating the photographs listed below from Ferrari and to Hugh Steward of Ferrari North America for initiating the arrangements to tour and take pictures of the Italian factories.

Gratitude is expressed to the following Ferrari owners who allowed their cars to be photographed and included in this book: Glenn Hanke for the 166 Inter on page 9; Al Cavey for the 365 GTB/4 Daytona on page 13, Tom and Tish Thinesen for the 246 GTS Dino on page 15, and Vern Zimmerman for the 328 GTB on page 31.

Thanks to Ken Parker for the drawing of Italy on page 4.

PHOTO CREDITS:

Ferrari: F40s on the cover and on pages 5, 28 and 29; Mondials on pages 24 and 25; Enzo Ferrari on pages 6-7; 250 Testa Rosa on page 10; 250 GTO on page 10; 365 GTB/4 Daytona on page 12; Berlinetta Boxer prototype on page 16; 328 GTS on pages 18-19; 500 F2 on page 20; F1 on page 21; 348s on page 22; and the Testarosa on pages 26-27.

Harry Haines: 166 Mille Miglia on page 8; 166 Inter on page 9; Pininfarina design emblem on page 11; 365 GTB Daytona on page 13; Dino prototype and Dino 246 GTS on pages 14-15; Berlinetta Boxer prototype and 512 BB on pages 16-17; Testarosa production line on page 27; and the 328 GTB with third graders Clay Estes and Christine Patterson on page 31.

Piero Ferrari: Enzo Ferrari on page 7.

Walter Iscara: Pope John Paul and F1 racing car on page 20.

Mazzi Flavio: Sylvester Stallone and 348s on page 22.

Library of Congress Cataloging-in-Publication Data

Haines, Shirley, 1935-
      Ferrari: the legend / by Shirley and Harry Haines.
         p. cm. – (Car classics)
      Includes index.
      Summary: Gives a brief history of the Ferrari automobile describing its special features and some classic models.
    ISBN 0-86593-146-1
    1. Ferrari automobile – Juvenile literature. [1. Ferrari automobile.]
I. Haines, Harry, 1932- . II. Title. III. Series: Car classics (Vero Beach, Fla.)
TL215.F47H35 1991
629.22'2–dc20
                            91-2088
                              CIP
                              AC

CONTENTS

CHAPTER 1

THE FERRARI IDEA

Ferraris are very unusual cars. First made in 1947, they have become legendary for their speed and beauty. The Italian government considers the Ferrari automobile a work of art and, in the summer of 1990, included it in a series of art exhibitions in Florence, Italy. This display was called "The Ferrari Idea." Many of the photographs in this book are from that exhibit.

Ferrari sports cars are very expensive. Year after year, they are among the highest priced cars in the world. One reason they are so costly is that they are considered works of art by many people.

One of the most famous trademarks in automobile history is the black prancing horse on a field of yellow with the Italian colors above.

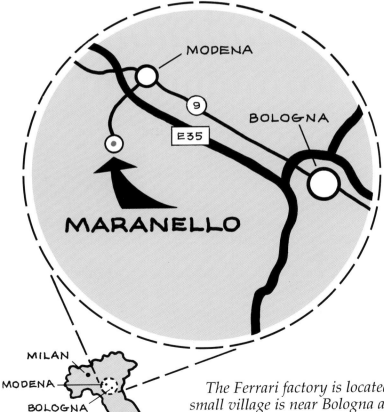

The Ferrari factory is located in Maranello, Italy. This small village is near Bologna and Modena, an area that is famous for high-performance autos.

Ferrari's top-of-the-line car for the 1990s, the model F40. It is sold only in the color red.

In a speech given at the opening of the Florence exhibition, "The Ferrari Idea" was described as having three parts:

1. The roar of a twelve-cylinder engine

2. The color red

3. The streamlined beauty of the bodywork

These three major qualities are so often true that the exceptions make interesting reading. An example is the model F40 pictured here. The streamlined beauty of the car seems clear. It is sold in only one color, red. What is the exception? It has a V-8 engine!

When the F40 was introduced in 1987, it road-tested at 201.3 mph and was called by many writers "the fastest car on the road." It is the fastest road car (not racing car) ever built by the Ferrari company.

CHAPTER 2

ENZO FERRARI

Enzo Ferrari built the company and is the man for whom the cars are named.

Rarely, if ever, has the history of a firm been so closely tied to the life of its founder.

Ferrari was born in Modena, Italy on February 18, 1898. Following World War I, he found a job with Alfa Romeo, the famous automobile company in Turin. He worked first as a mechanic, then as a test driver, later as a racing driver, and finally as sales manager.

World War II left Italy in shambles. May, 1945 found Enzo Ferrari trying to manufacture machine tools in his home town of Modena. In spite of all the hardship and poverty, Enzo saw this time as an opportunity to begin his dream, that of building cars under the name Ferrari. He used as his model E. Bugatti, probably the most famous car builder of the 1920s and 1930s. Bugatti tested his cars in the racing circuits; when he had a winner, he used the technology to produce spirited sports cars that sold for top prices. It was a proven formula, and it would work well for the new Ferrari company.

The first car that could really be called a Ferrari was test-run in Maranello, Italy on March 12, 1947. It was a two-seater sports car called the 125. The 125 won seven races that year, including the Rome Grand Prix. Next came the 166 series of Ferraris and many more racing victories. Rich and famous people from all over the world wanted sports cars built in the tiny shop in Maranello.

A young Enzo Ferrari in 1920, sitting behind the wheel of his Alfa Romeo Grand Prix racing car. With his mechanic Michele Conti, he drove this car in the Targa Florio, winning second place overall and first in his category.

Enzo Ferrari shortly before his death in 1988. Few men, if any, will be as remembered for their part in the history of the automobile. This rare photo was obtained from Enzo Ferrari's son, Piero.

Almost all of the cars of this era were powered by the Ferrari V-12 twin-six engine. It was an incredible feat that a small, almost backyard workshop could produce one of the world's most successful racing engines in this postwar era. While the company has over the years manufactured outstanding engines that have only 4, 6, or 8 cylinders, the V-12 is still the symbol for Ferrari's leadership in engine design.

Enzo Ferrari died on August 14, 1988 and was buried privately the following day. The company, now owned by Fiat, is more successful than ever and plans to produce about 4,000 cars per year at its plants in Maranello and Modena.

The 1931 Bobbio-Renice race was Ferrari's last victory as a driver. He is seen here with his mechanic Ongaro. In the early years of automobile racing, cars often suffered mechanical failure, and it was customary for each car to carry two men, a driver and a mechanic.

CHAPTER 3

THE FIRST FERRARIS: 1947-1949

Enzo Ferrari's approach to building cars was to make only the chassis and drive train – in other words, all of the car except the body. The bodies were manufactured by companies who specialized in custom bodywork. Pictured here are two cars that are mechanically the same but look quite different. Both were built in 1949 and have the same chassis and engine. Both are named model 166.

The blue two-seater is called the 166 Mille Miglia. It is probably one of the first two dozen cars built by Ferrari and is a classic example of the high performance and timeless elegance that made the company famous in the late 1940s. Its name, Mille Miglia, means "thousand miles" and comes from the celebrated 1,000-mile Italian race. This was the second car made by Ferrari to win the race, at that time the most famous in Italy and one of the most important in world-class racing. The body was designed and built by a company named Touring.

A 1949 model 166 Mille Miglia on display at the Florence exhibit, July, 1990. All Ferrari cars of this era were powered by a 60° V-12 engine, which was the finest racing motor of the day.

A 1949 model 166 Inter at the Concours d'Elegance in Pebble Beach, California, August, 1990. Bodywork was by Stabilimenti Farina. The serial #0041 indicates that it was probably the first Ferrari brought to the United States. Underneath the coupé body was a racing engine and chassis.

The red coupé is called a 166 Inter. Underneath its bodywork is the same engine and chassis that was winning the most famous races of the day. These two cars illustrate the original idea of Enzo Ferrari, which was to build road cars that were proven as racing cars. He continued to follow this idea for many years, until the changes in international racing rules became so restricted that Ferrari GT sports and road cars had to be made separately.

The Ferrari 166

years	1948-1950
number built	37
engine	V-12 60°
displacement	1995
compression	8.0:1
bhp	110 at 6000 rpm
transmission	5-speed w/reverse, non-synchromesh
top speed	120 mph
0 – 100 mph	27 seconds

CHAPTER 4

THE CAR THAT MADE FERRARI A LEGEND: THE 250

A 1959 model 250 Testa Rosa Spyder. This famous engine with a head that was painted red was noted for its six twin carburetors.

A 1964 250 GTO berlinetta. One of the first Ferraris to be designed in a wind tunnel, the GTO body forecast the "racer's wedge" profile that emerged later in the decade and reshaped virtually every racing car.

In 1947, Ferrari made three cars. Not three models, just three cars, period. By 1953 the company's total output for its entire seven-year history was only 189 automobiles. These cars were all custom made and included the 125 Sport, the 166 series, 195 and 212 Inter, 340 America, 342 America, 375 America, 410 Superamerica, and a number of variations of all those just mentioned.

The Ferrari 250 GTO	
years	1962-1964
number built	39
engine	V-12 60°
displacement	2953 cc
compression	9.8:1
bhp	280 at 7500 rpm
transmission	5-speed w/reverse, synchromesh
top speed	176 mph
0 – 100 mph	14.1 seconds

In 1954 Ferrari introduced the 250 GT. It was a production car that lasted for 10 years and made Ferrari a world-class automobile company. Over this period about 2,500 cars were made that could be called model 250. Two of the most famous are pictured here, the 250 Testa Rosa Spyder and the 250 GTO. By 1964, when the 250s ended, Ferrari was making 650 cars a year.

In Italian, *testa* means "head" and *rosa* is "red". The name Testa Rosa translates literally as "red head." The name started in the late 1950s because of a new, souped-up version of the Ferrari V-12 engine. A mechanic wanted to make sure the new power plant did not get mixed up with the other production engines, so he painted its head with red paint. In the following months as the new car with the powerful engine was being test driven, everyone called it Testa Rosa, and the name stuck. Twenty-five years later, when the new Ferrari with cheese-slicer vents was introduced, the company looked for a name that had become associated with their history. The name everyone liked was Testa Rosa, so it was combined it into one word, Testarosa, and has become one of the most famous car names in the world.

GTO, a term used by many car manufacturers today, originated with the Ferrari shown on the facing page. GT stands for *grande turismo*, translated in English as "grand touring." Touring was a term much used in the first half of the twentieth century for travel by automobile from city to city. Grand touring was merely touring in a grand style, the best. The O in GTO refers to the Italian word *omolgato*. Briefly, this means that enough cars were built of a particular model that it could be certified (to accommodate racing rules) as a production automobile rather than as a specialized racing car. So, a GTO is a grand touring car certified for racing.

In 1952 Ferrari decided his cars needed a more consistent appearance and determined that this would be possible only by using a single design company. He therefore entered into an agreement with Pininfarina. Since 1953 almost all Ferrari bodywork has been done by that firm; history has now shown this to be an outstanding partnership.

DISEGNO DI *pininfarina*

CHAPTER 5

THE BIG SELLER: DAYTONA

Named for the well-known race in Daytona, Florida, the model 365 GTB/4 was introduced by Ferrari at the Paris Auto Show in October of 1968. Its price was $20,000, and at that time it was the most expensive and fastest road car in Ferrari's 21-year history. The company claimed its top speed at 174 mph.

The most surprising feature of the new car was the size of its engine. It was a 4.4 liter, dohc V-12 with six Weber carburetors that produced 352 hp at 7500 rpm. For a 1968 sports car, these were big numbers. Even today, the Daytona is regarded as the most "macho" of all Ferraris.

In *Ferrari, the Man and His Machines*, Pete Lyons quotes an article in *l'Equipe* dated August 16, 1972. It gives a precise comparison of the Daytona, the Lamborghini Miura, the Mercedes 350SL, the Jaguar V-12 E-type, and the de Tomaso Pantera. At 172 mph, the Ferrari was the fastest of the five, ahead of the Miura (169 mph) and the Pantera (150

A 1968 GTB4 Daytona berlinetta. A berlinetta is a closed coupé body style, usually with seating for only two people.

A 1972 365 GTB/4 Daytona on display at a car rally in Carmel Valley, California August, 1990. The Daytona was the last of the line of great front-engine V-12 Ferraris and is still considered one of the finest cars ever produced.

mph). The much greater power of the Ferrari also gave it the best acceleration, with 13.8 seconds for a standing start to 400 meters and 24.3 seconds for a standing start kilometer. This compared to 14.3 and 25.5 seconds respectively for the Miura, its closest competitor.

Racing-modified Daytonas were known as big, brutal machines that relied on power for their speed. *Cavalino* magazine expressed it this way: "A Daytona at full clip was a sight to behold, mean looking and muscled, weaving dramatically on its overworked suspension, shaking and darting under heavy braking in a corner; literally pushing air and dust aside, leaving a wake and making its own weather." When Ferrari people talk about the roar of a 12-cylinder engine, they are most likely speaking of a Daytona.

The 365 GTB/4 Daytona

years	1968-1973
number built	1300
engine	V-12 (60°) front-engine
displacement	4390 cc
valve operation	dohc
compression	8.8:1
bhp	352 at 7500 rpm
transmission	5-speed w/reverse, synchromesh
top speed	174 mph
0 – 100 mph	18.3 seconds

CHAPTER 6

NAMED FOR HIS SON: THE DINO SERIES

Enzo Ferrari named his first son Alfredino, after his father, and then shortened the name to the affectionate form, Dino. As a young man Dino was an excellent engineering student, and he was welcomed into the company. In the early 1950s, it seemed obvious that he was being groomed to inherit the business that his father had built.

Dino was given the authority to develop a new racing engine, and he made a surprising choice for the basic design. It was a V-6. But the promising young Ferrari never got to hear the engine run. He died of kidney failure in June, 1956, when he was only 26.

Dino's death crushed Enzo. In his autobiography, published six years later, the elder Ferrari states, "the only perfect love in this world is that of a father for his son." He named the GT 206 and 246 cars Dino rather than Ferrari. There was no prancing horse emblem on any of the cars during the models' eight-year production run.

The 1967 Dino prototype. This was a Formula One racing car, but it was only a short step away from the road car shown opposite. Its aerodynamics were the most advanced of the day and symbolic of the close relationship between Ferrari design and racing.

With a small light body and the powerful V-6 engine mounted in the rear, the Dino was reported to be incredibly agile. Its design elements were strikingly beautiful and forecast the direction of sports car shapes for years to come.

A 1972 246 GTS Dino on display at a car rally in Carmel Valley, California in August, 1990. This was the first Ferrari with a V-6 mid-engine. In 1970 it cost $13,400.

The Dino 246 GT/GTS

years	1969-1974
number built	4000 plus
engine	V-6 (65°) transverse mid-engine
displacement	2418 cc
compression	9.0:1
bhp	195 at 7600 rpm
transmission	5-speed w/reverse, synchromesh
top speed	146 mph
0 – 100 mph	9 seconds

CHAPTER 7

ENGINE-IN-THE-REAR:
THE BERLINETTA BOXER

Prototype of the Berlinetta Boxer BB as it was first presented at the 1971 Turin Motor Show. The word "boxer" referred to a flat engine with the cylinders opposed.

All cars have characteristics for which they are noted. Some have a single trait that makes them stand out in history. For the Ferrari Berlinetta Boxer, this singular characteristic was the engine. It had two banks of six cylinders positioned horizontally, opposing one another from opposite sides of the crankshaft. Often called "flat" engines, they are also nicknamed "boxers" because of the pistons punching at each other from opposite sides.

Above left: A front shot taken at a car rally in Monterey, California August, 1990. The air dam underneath the front bumper identifies this model as a 512 BB.

Above right: The view most often seen of a Berlinetta Boxer. This photograph of the original prototype was taken at the Florence exhibit, July 1990.

The engine for this car had been tested in Formula One racing for almost a decade before it was first offered to the public in 1973. According to Mel Nichols, who interviewed the project engineers for his book, *Ferrari Berlinetta Boxer*, the development motor produced 380 horsepower at 7000 rpm. This was nearly 30 more horsepower than the same size V-12, and at 500 rpm less. Nichols said the engine started with "a fierce, stunning bark like that of a Formula One engine except that the beat that followed was steady and free of the popping and spluttering of the race-car engine. Nor was the noise quite so savagely loud. But it had an awesome wail, deep and unmistakably the end product of enormous strength. Even those used to the marvellous sound of multi-cylinder (Ferrari) engines tended to sit and listen to it for a few minutes, marvelling."

A major part of the car's success was the way it looked. Very low (3.68 feet) and wide (5.91 feet), it looked like a car that was 25 years ahead of its time. Its dominant styling feature was the line around the entire car that separated the lower panels at about the top of the wheel rims. The lower panels were always black, no matter what color the car.

The performance and sheer animal magnetism of the Berlinetta Boxer were the best, and it also exerted another kind of power. It made engine-in-the-rear technology a Ferrari standard. The company has not produced a front-engine road car series since.

The Berlinetta Boxer BB

years	1971-1984
number built	NA
engine	flat 12 (boxer) in the rear
displacement	4942 cc
valve operation	dohc
compression	9.2:1
bhp	360 at 6200 rpm
transmission	5-speed w/reverse, synchromesh
top speed	188 mph
0 – 100 mph	10 seconds

CHAPTER 8

MAGNUM P.I.'S FERRARI: THE 328 GTS

Most people have never seen a Ferrari in person, but those who have are unlikely to forget it. Of course any automobile changes over the years, but people tend to remember an outstanding model and build their mental image on it. Such is the case of the Ferrari 328, for two reasons. It was the largest production Ferrari of its era and therefore the most visible. The 328 has been shown repeatedly on television, most often on the series "Magnum P.I." When the average person tries to describe a Ferrari, he probably pictures the car shown here.

The 328 series was Ferrari's best seller in the 1980s. When introduced in 1986, the American version MSRP was $64,393.

Probably the most famous car on TV in the 1980s, this Ferrari 328 GTS was frequently seen on the TV series "Magnum P.I."

The 328 GTB

years	1986-1989
number built	approximately 5400
engine	V-8 90° transverse mid-engine
displacement	3186 cc
valve operation	dohc, 4 valves per cylinder
compression	9.2:1
bhp	260 at 7000 rpm
transmission	5-speed w/reverse, synchromesh
top speed	156 mph
0 – 100 mph	15.9 seconds

The producers of "Magnum P.I." needed a car for Tom Selleck, their series star, and they wanted a sexy, expensive sports car. It had to be suitable for a millionaire's estate on Hawaii. The series was a hit, and one of their most memorable props was the Ferrari.

Writing in the May, 1986 issue of *Car and Driver*, Tony Assenza noted that the 328 "has one of the world's best V-8s, inspired looks, a fine suspension, and a lock on about two-thirds of the world's automotive magic."

The 328 was discontinued in 1989 to make way for its successor, the 348.

CHAPTER 9

RACING CARS

"The will to win and to be seen doing so" was the driving spirit behind Enzo Ferrari and his company. Over the second half of the twentieth century, no other name has become so widely associated with racing in the general public's mind.

In 1929 Enzo Ferrari organized Scuderia Ferrari, a group of gentlemen drivers who joined together to compete as a team in weekend motor races. Enzo's passion for racing thrived during the 1930s through these team projects. In 1947, when his company produced its first car under the name Ferrari, it was a racing car. It won seven races in its first year, including the Rome Grand Prix. In the years since, Ferraris have competed in virtually every race in the world racing circuit and have won prizes too numerous to list.

Ferrari racing cars are of enormous interest to everyone. Even Pope John Paul makes a visit to the Maranello factory to view Ferrari's latest.

The two racing cars pictured here represent Ferrari racing technology now spanning almost half a century. The 1952 model 500 type is one of the most famous racing cars in history and produced Ferrari's first world championship in Formula One. The 1989 model 640 type has led the way in non-turbo racing technology. Ferrari is using this car and its successors to try multi-valve cylinder heads (the model 641 has 5 valves per cylinder), the reduction of internal friction, and weight reduction through lightweight materials such as carbon fiber.

The 1952 model 500 F2 is a legend. This car won every race it entered during 1952 and 1953. Driver Alberto Ascari used the car to win the world championship both years. Its in-line 4-cylinder engine was a new departure in racing technology.

These new experiments will eventually find their way into sports cars intended for the highway, not the racetrack. That was the original "Ferrari Idea." It was central to the life of Enzo Ferrari and continues today with the company that bears his name.

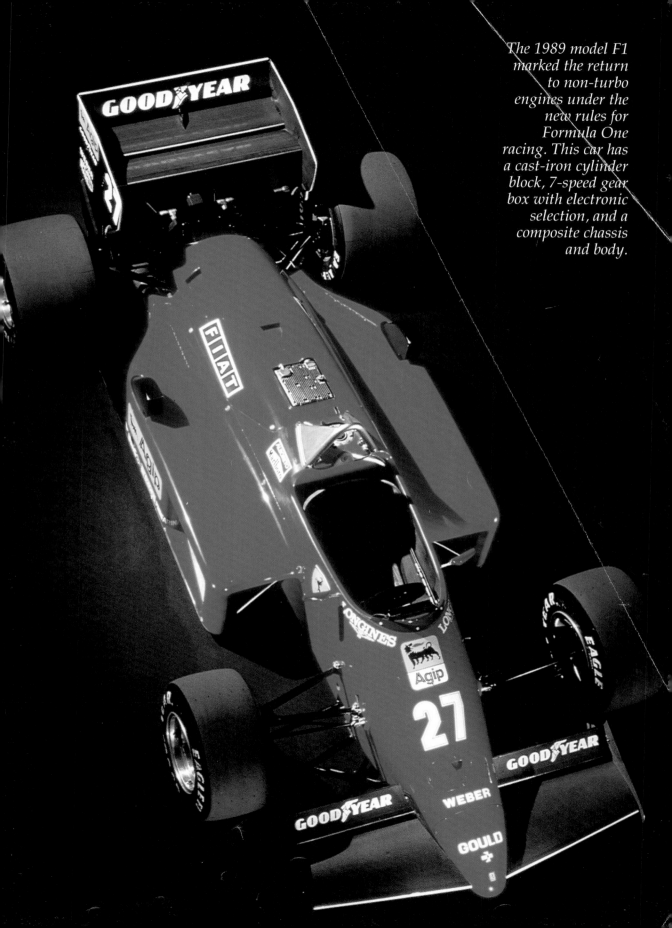

The 1989 model F1 marked the return to non-turbo engines under the new rules for Formula One racing. This car has a cast-iron cylinder block, 7-speed gear box with electronic selection, and a composite chassis and body.

CHAPTER 10

A CAR FOR THE 90S: THE 348

If any Ferrari can be called a standard model, it would be the 348. First introduced in the 1990s, it is the mainline, two-seater sports car. The model number follows Ferrari's current system of using the first two numbers to indicate engine size and the last digit to show the number of cylinders. Thus, a 348 has an engine of 3.4 liters with 8 cylinders.

The 348 is a direct descendant of the Dino, and its history can be traced as follows:

MODEL	CC	TYPE	YEAR
Dino 206	2.0	V-6	1967
Dino 246	2.4	V-6	1969
Dino 308 2+2	3.0	V-8	1973
Ferrari	3.0	V-8	1975
Ferrari 308 Quatro	3.0	V-8	1982
Ferrari 328	3.2	V-8	1986
Ferrari 348	3.4	V-8	1990

Sylvester Stallone at the factory in Maranello looking over the selection of 348s.

The 348 comes in two models: the berlinetta (called the "tb") and the removable targa top (called the "ts"). The 348 is Ferrari's successor to the 328 and probable best seller for the 1990s.

The 348 has several features that are similar to the Testarosa, and it is sometimes confused with the larger, more expensive car. The most obvious of these similarities is the horizontal grill on the doors. Large engines in the rear demand great amounts of air for cooling. The cheese-slicer air intakes provided the answer to this technical problem and, as so often happens at Ferrari, created a new Ferrari styling theme. This new design will probably be copied by other cars in the 1990s.

The 348tb or 348ts

years	1990 to current
number built	in production
engine	V-8 90° mid-engine
displacement	3405 cc
valve operation	4 overhead camshafts, 4 valves per cylinder
compression	10.4:1
bhp	300 at 7200 rpm
transmission	5-speed w/reverse, synchromesh
top speed	above 172 mph
0 – 62 mph (100 km)	5.6 seconds
standing kilometer	24.7 seconds

CHAPTER 11

FOUR-SEATER FERRARI: THE MONDIAL

The Mondial is Ferrari's only convertible and only car with seating for four.

Most Ferraris are two-seater sports cars with roofs. If you want a bit of open-air driving, you can always choose the 348ts, with removable targa top. But if you want a full convertible or if you need seating for four, there is only one choice: the Mondial. Its Pininfarina design is a very nice solution to the challenges of a mid-engine four-seat design. While its performance is no match for the other current models, which are all high-performance two-seaters, the Mondial is a big seller. Many car experts also report that it is the sweetest model to drive.

The Mondial	
years	1980 to current
number built	in production (approximately 500 per year)
engine	V-8 90° mid-engine
displacement	207.1 cubic inches
valve operation	4 overhead camshafts, 4 valves per cylinder
compression	10.4:1
DIN hp	221 at 7200 rpm
transmission	5-speed w/reverse, synchromesh
top speed	158.4 mph
0 – 62 mph (100 km)	6.3 seconds
standing kilometer	25.8 seconds

First introduced in 1980, the original car, called the Mondial 8, consisted of the 308 GTB engine and chassis with an added rear seat and Pininfarina body. Given the 3.2 liter V-8 from the 328 GTB, it became the Mondial 3.2 in 1982. A cabriolet version was introduced in 1983.

The Mondial has to be one of the most technically innovative automobiles to be produced by the cooperation of Ferrari and Pininfarina. Its 2+2 seating with a powerful engine mounted behind the passengers is a remarkable triumph of both engineering and design. It is able to lumber around town in almost any gear, yet go like a bullet when out on the road where performance is needed.

The slowest Ferrari has a top speed of "only" 158.4 mph. With production starting in 1980, it is also the oldest design. But its lower price and extra seats make it a bigger seller than either the Testarosa or F40.

CHAPTER 12

FERRARI WITH 12 CYLINDERS: THE TESTAROSA

Introduced in 1984 at the Paris Auto Show, the Testarosa was first produced as a 1985 model. It was the first Ferrari created especially for the American market after the U.S. instituted safety and emission laws. This car bears no resemblance to its namesake, the Testa Rosa V-12 racing car (the original name was two words), except that the head of the engine is red.

The Testarosa is Ferrari's only 12-cylinder car in current production. It was an outgrowth of boxer technology and uses a refined version of the engine that made the Berlinetta Boxer famous. After the cheese-slicer sides, the most striking impression of the car is one of enormous width. The body measures 77.8 inches across, making it the largest Ferrari and nearly seven inches wider than the contemporary Corvette.

The Testarosa is perhaps the most stylistically memorable car ever produced by Ferrari because of the cheese-slicer air vents on the side. Measuring a huge 77.8 inches across yet only 44.5 high, the Testarosa is one of the world's widest and lowest cars. Its low center of gravity results in excellent handling.

Pininfarina, the designer, used their full-size wind tunnel to develop the car's shape. Extensive testing produced exceptional down-force at the front and rear, eliminating the need for spoilers. The long air-intake troughs were found to be necessary for engine cooling and were also developed in the wind tunnel.

The Testarosa is a classic Ferrari in that it combines the best of mechanical, styling, and aerodynamic technology for automobiles.

The Testarosa production line at the factory in Maranello, Italy. This facility is remarkable for its spotlessly clean environment.

Ferrari Testarosa	
years	1985 to current
number built	in production
engine	boxer 12-cylinder mid-engine
displacement	4943 cc
valve operation	dohc, 4 valves per cylinder
compression	8.8:1
bhp	390 at 6800 rpm
transmission	5-speed w/reverse, synchromesh
top speed	181 mph
0 – 100 mph	11.2 seconds

CHAPTER 13

TOP-OF-THE-LINE FERRARI: THE F40

The unveiling of the F40 occurred at a moving ceremony in Maranello, Italy on July 21, 1987. Dennis Simanaitis wrote about it in *Road and Track* magazine:

> The hall was filled to overflowing with a goodly number of the world's automotive press. Ferrari staff people milled around; for some reason or other, it wasn't quite time to begin. But then a commotion at the side entrance made it all clear; Enzo Ferrari, the Old Man, a patriarch loved and respected, moved to his central position at the speaker's table amid applause from journalists and company people alike. His walk was stately, slow and not entirely firm, but when he spoke, his voice betrayed none of the frailty that you would expect of 89 years.
>
> "Little more than a year ago," he said through an English interpreter, "I expressed my wish to the engineers. Build a car to be the best in the world. And now the car is here."
>
> With that, the red covering was swept aside to reveal another red shape beneath. Applause erupted and, for a time, no words were spoken. Photographers swarmed around the starkly lit car.
>
> "*Bello, molto bello*," I heard a voice say softly. Then I realized that Enzo Ferrari's microphone had been accidentally left on.

Top view of the top-rated Ferrari. While many aspects of this car are unusual, none is more surprising than the clear plastic body over the engine. Of course, not many cars have an engine to show off like the F40. The entire body is made of composite materials.

The F40 gets its name from the year it was introduced, 1987, the fortieth year of Ferrari as an auto maker. Its V-8 engine makes possible a more compact and lighter car. These qualities have made the F40 a world leader in speed, agility, and responsiveness.

The last car of Enzo Ferrari's life was not only "beautiful, very beautiful," it was fast, very fast. The factory claim was 0 to 60 mph in 3.5 seconds and a top speed of 201.3 mph. The F40 was reportedly the first production sports car to surpass 200 mph and is, even today, one of only two or three automobiles to be so acknowledged by the press.

The F40 is the spectacular result of the Ferrari evolution of a GTO car. It is today "the ultimate Ferrari"!

For years, red has been the traditional color for Ferrari. With this model the company made it official. The F40 comes only in red. It has huge tires and giant 13-inch brake rotors. All that tread and stopping-power was made necessary by the F40's engine.

Ferrari F40

years	1987 to current
number built	in production
engine	V-8 90° longitudinal mid-engine
displacement	2326 cc
valve operation	dohc, 4 valves per cylinder
compression	7.7:1
bhp	478 at 7000 rpm
transmission	5-speed w/reverse, synchromesh
top speed	201.3 mph
0 – 60 mph	3.5 seconds

CHAPTER 14

FERRARI: IMPORTANT DATES

1898 Enzo Ferrari born in Modena, Italy, February 18.

1908 Alfredo Ferrari, Sr., takes his son Enzo, age 10, to Bologna car races. Vincenzo Lancia sets fastest lap.

1914 World War I begins; Enzo's father and brother both die in military service. Enzo is drafted to serve in a mountain artillery unit.

1919 Enzo Ferrari's first race as a driver; he finishes fourth in the Parma-Berceto driving a CMN.

1920 Enzo Ferrari employed by Alfa Romeo, a relationship that lasts almost 20 years.

1924 Ferrari wins the Coppa Acerbo race and is named "Cavaliere" (equivalent to knighthood) by the Italian government. Prancing horse emblem is used.

1929 Scuderia Ferrari (translated as "Ferrari Team") is organized. This is a group of racing enthusiasts headed by Enzo Ferrari.

1930 Alfredino Ferrari, first son of Enzo Ferrari, is born.

1932 Scuderia Ferrari dominates Grand Prix racing using modified Alfa Romeo cars.

1939 Scuderia Ferrari ends; Ferrari severs ties with Alfa Romeo and sets up a manufacturing and design firm in Modena to make automobile tools and parts.

1940 Mussolini declares Italy at war, joins partners with Germany and Japan against the Allies.

1945 War ends. Ferrari now owns a small manufacturing shop located a few miles south of Modena in the village of Maranello.

1947 The first Ferrari, model 125, is test run in Maranello on March 12. It has a superb V-12 engine.

1947 A Ferrari car enters its first race at Piacenza, May 11. Leading just two laps from the finish, the fuel pump fails and the car is forced out of the race.

1949 Ferrari wins its first Formula One race, the Grand Prix of Rosario. The first Ferraris are sold in America. A Ferrari wins Europe's most famous race, the Le Mans 24-hour competition.

1952 Alberto Ascari wins the first world championship in a Formula One Ferrari.

1956 Alfredino "Dino" Ferrari, Enzo's son, dies of kidney failure at age 26.

1960 Experiments begin with engine behind the driver.

1961 Phil Hill wins the world championship in a mid-engine Ferrari.

1962 The GTO is introduced through a loophole in racing rules and wins many races.

1963 Ferrari wins Le Mans race with the 250P, a sports-racer with V-12 engine in the rear.

1965 The 250LM wins Le Mans, the last victory at this race during Enzo Ferrari's lifetime.

1967 A team of Ferrari P4s finish 1-2-3 at Daytona.

1968 The 365 GTB/4 Daytona is first shown at the Paris Auto Show.

1969 Fiat purchases 40 percent of Ferrari and takes over the production car manufacturing.

1971 Berlinetta Boxer introduced at the Turin Motor Show.

1975 Model 308 GTB, a car that will later become the 328 and then 348, is introduced at the Paris Auto Show.

1980 The first Mondial, a 2+2 called model 8, is introduced at the Geneva Auto Show.

1983 Mondial cabriolet, Ferrari's only current convertible, begins production.

1984 Testarosa shown at Paris Auto Show.

1985 Model 328 GTB, Ferrari's largest production car of the 1980s, is introduced at the Frankfurt Auto Show.

1987 The F40 is introduced on the company's fortieth anniversary at a moving ceremony in Maranello, July 21.

1988 Enzo Ferrari dies, August 14.

1990 Model 348 introduced as successor to the 328.

1990 "The Ferrari Idea," an exhibition in Florence sponsored by the Italian government, runs June 8 through September 30.

GLOSSARY

berlinetta (bair-lee-NET-a) – A closed-coupé body style.

Bologna (boh-LOAN-yah) – A city in northern Italy.

cabriolet (CAB-ree-o-lay) – A car with a canvas top that can be folded down, a convertible.

cc – Cubic centimeters. The amount of space in the engine cylinders. The larger the number of cubic centimeters, the larger the engine and power.

dohc – Dual overhead cam. Two drives (instead of one) that operate the levers or cams that open and close the valves and are located over the head of the engine.

km/h – Kilometers per hour. The speed of a car in kilometers.

Mille Miglia (MEE-lay MEEL-yah) – A thousand miles. The name of a famous race in Italy which is 1,000 miles in length.

Modena (MOWED-n-eh) – The Italian city where Enzo Ferrari was born.

mph – Miles per hour. The speed of a car in miles.

MSRP – Manufacturer's suggested retail price. While cars are rarely sold for this amount, this figure is probably the best for comparison cost analysis.

Pininfarina (PEE-neen-fah-REE-nah) – The Italian coach-building company that has designed almost all Ferraris since 1953.

synchromesh (SIN-crow-mesh) – A gearbox design that helps to align the gears of an auto and makes shifting easier and smoother.

INDEX